LIONS

KING OF BEASTS

Lee Server

NEW LINE BOOKS

Fax: (888) 719-7723
e-mail: info@newlinebooks.com

Printed and bound in Singapore

ISBN 1-59764-131-6

Visit us on the web!
www.newlinebooks.com

Author: Lee Server

Producer: Robert M. Tod
Book Designer: Mark Weinberg
Editor: Mary Forsell
Photo Editor: Natasha Milne
Design Associate: Jackie Skroczky

TABLE OF CONTENTS

INTRODUCTION

The majestic lion is the legendary ruler of the animal kingdom. Revered for its strength and bravery, the lion has been a symbol of supremacy since the beginning of recorded history.

How did the lion ascend to the throne in a kingdom full of fierce contenders? It is not the largest of animals. Measured in full length, the average male lion is no larger than 10 feet (3.1 meters) from nose to tail. It is not the strongest of animals, nor the fastest. Its skills as a hunter are, in fact, deeply flawed. With its plain brown or sandy body coloration and tufted tail, the lion also does not by any means possess the most beautiful coat nor rival the plumage of other animals in its habitat.

And yet its position remains nearly uncontested. Certainly, there are few human observers who have seen a full-grown lion in the wild who would ever question its supremacy. It has much to do with bearing. The lion conveys grandeur and self-assurance. This is particularly true of a grown male, which possesses a magnificent mane, so much like a king's ceremonial headdress or an Indian chief's war bonnet. There is the undoubted fierceness of the lion in battle and in destroying its prey. And there is that roar, a low grumble building in intensity, used to signify territoriality and power. The lion has learned how to make this roar send a vibrating signal throughout its domain, literally making the earth quake. And then, equally impressive, is the lion's catlike aura of intelligence, conveying a sense of subtle thought processes at work. For such things and more does the lion justly claim its crown.

The lion has long been a symbol of superiority. The lion's body is the basis for the Egyptian sphinx, which has the head of a human, ram, or hawk. Usually representing courage and domination, the lion is a symbolic motif in the Bible and also appears in many folk tales, including Aesop's fables. Throughout this century, the lion's image has appeared frequently, associated with every-

thing from sports teams to men's clubs to insurance companies. Even the movie industry has employed the lion's image: Beginning in the 1920s, Leo the Lion became the impressive corporate symbol for Metro-Goldwyn-Mayer, the Hollywood studio.

Despite the lion's exalted status, man has made this animal's continued existence a problem in some cases and an impossibility in others. Various lion subspecies once roamed across large stretches of Europe and Asia. But the growing hordes of humankind, with their need to expand their domain and to tame the wilderness, successfully chased several lion subspecies right into extinction. In other cases, vast lion populations were reduced—through hunting, habitat loss, and other factors—to a small, lonely enclave. Were it not for the efforts in this century of a tiny number of prescient and dedicated conservationists, both professional and amateur, even more damage might have been done.

As of this writing, the lion is not an officially labeled "endangered species." African governments have made great improvements in maintaining national parks and sanctuaries and in protecting the animals residing there from hunters and poachers. The old days of massive lion-hunting safaris, when mostly visiting amateur "sportsmen" wounded or killed countless thousands of lions, are no more.

Lions in captivity now thrive and breed freely in their unusual surroundings. Furthermore, scientific research into the genetics of particular lion subspecies may eventually help to increase the number of lions in the wild by introducing captive-raised lions to that environment. And in India, naturalists continue to work to increase that continent's one and only remaining population of Asiatic lions, hoping to successfully introduce the subspecies beyond their current single, small enclave in the Gir National Park and Lion Sanctuary.

But in a world where wilderness habitat is lost to the tractor every minute of every day, where governments feel they must put their ambitions and their expanding human population's needs ahead of a wild animal's right to exist, and where numerous species come close to extinction each year, it would be naive to believe the lion's future is entirely certain. Various organizations in Africa, the United States, and around the world must work throughout the year just to prevent the world's lion population from losing any more ground.

In the following pages, we will explore the

origins of these magnificent monarchs of the wild, as well as the colorful family tree of all the cats, determining how much the fierce lion has in common with its cousin the common, domesticated feline. We will examine the distinctive nature of lions—their methods of hunting, mating, and raising cubs. Lions are the only sociable cat, living not alone or in pairs like other cats, but in large, familial groups called "prides." Examining the pride's intricate social hierarchy, we will see that life for a lion family member can involve both selfish brutality and great kindness and generosity.

The text will also chart the sometimes inspiring but too often violent and destructive relationship between lion and man. Demonizing the lion as a man-eating monster allowed for the senseless "sporting" slaughter of whole lion prides. But in one case, at least, recalled in detail herein—the story of Elsa the Lioness, and Joy and George Adamson—the relationship between lion and man proved to be constructive and mutually respectful.

In our tour of lion country, we will also examine the various animal reserves where lions can be viewed in the wild and learn of the field and lab work being done to ensure that the lion's future will be a bright one.

THE HISTORY OF THE LION

Lions are members of the cat family, whose original ancestors date back some twelve million years. The various types of cats have actually changed very little in all of that time.

The proper family name for cats is Felidae. Under this family heading are three genera, or groupings, of cats: *Panthera*, *Acinonyx*, and *Felis*. The fast-moving cheetah, native to Africa and large parts of eastern and southern Asia, is the only member of the *Acinonyx* group. The *Felis* group includes all the smaller cats, both wild and domestic, from *F. concolor* (the fierce American puma or mountain lion) to *F. catus* (the common domestic cat). The remaining cats all belong to the *Panthera* genus. These include the big cats of legend, the roaring royalty of the jungle, forest, and savannah: the leopard (*P. pardus*) and its variants, the snow leopard (*P. uncia*) and clouded leopard (*P. nebulosa*); the tiger (*P. tigris*); and, of course, wildlife's uncontested king, the lion (*P. leo*).

Despite their very different worlds and ways of living, the various groups of cats remain close cousins in a variety of ways. Unlikely as it would first seem, the untamed African lion has much in common with the pampered pussycat curled up in a suburban living room. Those observing lions in the wild are often struck by how frequently the huge and dangerous animals re-create the poses and personality traits of a pet tabby. Similarly, the housecat, domesticated only a mere four thousand years ago (a fraction of the time that the dog has been domesticated), has retained hunting instincts and other feral abilities that link it to the regal lion.

As for the lion, natural scientists are only now just beginning to understand the capacity for diversity and adaptation of which the King of Beasts is capable.

FROM PREHISTORIC TIMES TO THE PRESENT

It was only in recent times that lions became known as animals of Africa. In bygone centuries, they could be found even more widely throughout Africa and in many other lands, including Europe and Asia. A species known as the cave lion lived in Europe during the late Ice Age. Profiles of lions were etched into the walls of caves in France more than fifteen thousand years ago.

Since the advent of recorded history, the lion has not existed in the wild anywhere in Europe, with the exception of Greece. Lions were reported as common in that country in 500 B.C., but by 300 B.C., Aristotle described them as being rare, and by A.D. 100, there were no further recorded sightings of lions in Greece. They did continue to exist in Palestine for many more centuries, finally disappearing from that region at the time of the Crusades.

To understand the history of the lion, it is necessary to understand the conditions that it needs to exist. Despite its reputation as the King of the Jungle, the lion actually does not inhabit jungles, nor does it live in very dry deserts or in the rain forests. Instead, the lion exists in what is termed scrub country.

It lives in some areas that have intense heat, but it also exists in some locales with cool climates. In fact, lion tracks have been found on Mount Kenya at altitudes of more than 2 miles (3.2 kilometers). But in most cases, it lives among grassy plains and thorny scrub trees. Historically, as the areas it inhabits have lost these characteristics, the lion has departed or has been driven out.

The lion's exit from Europe in prehistoric times was most likely the result of the massive spreading of forests throughout the continent, making the area uninhabitable for this animal. In the more recent past, we can clearly survey the

shrinking distribution of the world's lion population, its total disappearance from areas it once called home in India, the Middle East (including Iran and northern Africa), and in parts of southern Africa. In all of these cases, mankind was directly responsible for the elimination of the lions or of the lions' habitat. As populations increased in the above areas, wilderness became towns and farmland, eliminating open grass and scrub. And as the lion lost its habitat to the plow, it increasingly lost its life to human weaponry. By the time of the invention of the high-powered hunting rifle, the lion had basically lost any chance of maintaining its homeland.

VANISHED SUBSPECIES

The vanished subspecies include the Cape lion, which roamed through southern Africa from the Cape of Good Hope to the province of Natal until cultivation of the land and hunting by emigrants caused its extinction. The last known Cape lion expired in 1865. The Barbary lion, once native to all of northern Africa from Morocco to Egypt, survived into the twentieth century. The last pure member of the subspecies was shot in Morocco in 1860, although traces of the bloodlines of the Barbary are still carried by some lions in captivity. The Persian lion, which was found in Asia Minor and the Transcaucasian range, disappeared by 1930. Almost all remaining lions are now sub-Saharan African subspecies. Among the surviving African breeds are the Masai lion, which lives in central-eastern Africa. The Senegalese lion is found in western Africa. Other subspecies on the continent include the Angolan and Rhodesian lions, as well as the Transvaal lion, found in South Africa's Kruger National Park.

Despite their survival and relatively healthy numbers at this point in time, the African lions have not had an easy time of it. Like the Asiatic lions, the Africans have been the target of hunters for centuries, and have seen even their vast wilderness become tamed by an increasing human population and its need to cultivate and exploit anything in its path. Luckily for the African lion, man's increasing attention to conservation and nations' growing awareness of the value of wildlife in attracting tourists have combined to give these lions a last-minute stay of execution. Nowadays, large stretches of African wilderness are established as protected wildlife reserves or parks. Traveling in vehicles within the parks, tourists can observe lion prides going about their lives in an almost perfectly natural state.

THE LIONS OF GIR

Sadly, as we have observed, the once wide-ranging lion population has shrunk almost entirely to a few regions on a single continent, Africa. This narrowing of the lion's domain has been going on since the last century, so it is not surprising that the average person thinks of the east or central African landscape as this animal's natural homeland. But there is one remaining exception to this rule, and it is such an odd and interesting occurrence that it deserves special attention.

The Indian lion is another regional name for the Asiatic lion, or *Panthera leo persica*, the subspecies that once ranged from Greece in the west to the far eastern regions of the Indian subcontinent. This lion has played a part in the symbols and folklore of Indian culture for more than two thousand years.

The Indian lion has long been celebrated as the Lord of Beasts, and it became a symbol for human power and sovereignty. In ancient societies in India, combat with a lion was considered the ultimate test of leadership. This gradually shifted to a safer, symbolic gesture of a leader cloaking himself in or standing upon a lion skin. There were magnificent depictions of lions on the statuary at Mahabalipuram. The most important symbolic use of the lion was associated with the Emperor Asoka in Sarnath, two thousand years ago. This depiction of a lion, symbolizing strength and power, eventually became the symbol for the modern Republic of India.

As India's population grew and began cultivating or settling more and more of its forest and scrublands, the Indian lion was squeezed nearly out of existence. Early in the century, the Gir Forest area in the state of Gujarat on the west coast was afflicted with a terrible famine—one so devastating that it is still mentioned in the folklore of the region. Because of the strained circumstances, the lion population began preying on the humans in the area. This prompted a massive backlash against the lions, resulting in a population of fewer than two dozen of the big cats by 1910.

Before they were completely wiped out, the Gir lions came under the protection of the Nawab of Junagadh, a local monarch who banned all lion hunting in the area. Soon, the lion population began to increase in number. By the time of Indian independence in 1947, the government had come to realize the importance and fragile nature of this last bastion of the Indian lion and the Nawab's conservation policy was upheld. Naturalists were assigned to study and take a census of the Gir's lion populace. At that time, there were more than 200 lions. Today, this number has increased to 250 lions.

The Indian government then created the Gir National Park and Lion Sanctuary, covering 540 square miles (1,404 square kilometers). The area is made up of dry scrubland with hills, rivers, and teak forest. In addition to its lion population, the Gir contains panthers, antelope, sambar, jackals, hyenas, and marsh crocodiles.

The lions of India are just slightly smaller than those of Africa, although the largest Indian lion on record was an imposing 9.6 feet (2.9 meters). The Indian lion is shaggier than its African cousin, with thicker fur on the coat and belly and a longer tail tuft. Oddly, though, the mane on the

male Indian lion is generally not as long as that of the African.

Naturalists have found no major behavioral differences between the Indian and African lions—with one important exception. The lions of Gir must share some of their territory with cattle and buffalo herdsmen. While the lions frequently attack the cattle in their midst, they have shown little aggressiveness toward humans. There are only a handful of instances of the lions coming into conflict with the local human population in the past thirty years. This is especially noteworthy considering that the park is somewhat crowded and the lions have occasionally roamed as far afield as the outskirts of nearby cities.

But this is not to say that the circumstances are ideal for the continued well-being of the Gir lions. The human population continues to encroach on the lions' territory and alter their habitat. Because the herdsmen bring their cattle through the park, their animals compete for space and food with the resident ungulate animals (largely herbivorous hoofed mammals), the lion's natural prey. Under the circumstances, the natural prey population cannot increase.

The Indian government has attempted to relieve the situation, but without much success as yet. It has erected walls around the core sanctuary to keep out grazing cattle, but this has been inef-fective. The government has attempted to relocate some of the people of the Gir, but this, too, has proven to be difficult to enforce. There have been attempts to relocate some Gir lions in other parts of India. In 1957, three of the lions were introduced into another protected area, the Chandraprabha Reserve in Uttar Pradesh. The lions did not multiply as hoped. Other lions were brought to the protected lands of the Maharajah of Varanasi, with similar results.

The most recent effort on the government's part has centered on the hills of Barda in the Porbandar region. The Indian government has set aside a 70-square-mile (182-square-kilometer) area for this potential second lion reserve. Lions had not lived in the Barda hills for more than eighty years, due to human encroachment and lack of prey animals. It will take many years before we know if the Barda will become another thriving enclave for the limited populace of Indian lions.

For now, the Gir National Park and Lion Sanctuary is the only place to see Asiatic lions in the wild, and the Indian government has begun to do more to make this unique spectacle visible to tourists and wildlife enthusiasts. The Gir Forest Department arranges weekly shows in which the lions are drawn into view with a buffalo lure. Guided Jeep safaris through the Gir are also available for observing lions. Because the lions are not afraid, or readily angered by the presence of people or vehicles, these safaris can offer very intimate views of the animals. Sometimes the lions actually approach and look over a vehicle in their midst.

As in African game reserves, the best time to observe the lions is at dawn and dusk. They are also frequently spotted following cattle being driven home, attacking any strays. The sanctuary is closed to the public from June to October. October and November are the primary mating months for the lions of Gir.

For those visitors unlucky enough not to sight a lion in the sanctuary, there is a last chance at the Junagadh Zoo at Sakar Bagh, a few miles from the center of town. There, six Gir lions live in apparent contentment alongside tigers, leopards, and the zoo's other star attractions.

THE NATURE OF THE LION

In size, the lion is second only to the tiger among members of the cat family. The male lion's weight usually ranges from 350 to 400 pounds (157 to 180 kilograms), though some individuals have been as heavy as 500 pounds (225 kilo-grams). The female lions are 250 to 300 pounds (112.5 to 135 kilograms). The normal length of the male is 9 feet (2.7 meters), while the females are usually about 8 feet (2.4 meters) long.

The coloration of lions does not vary by gender. All lions are a yellowish tan color, also described as a sandy buff. One of the advantages of this hue for the lion is that it is able to hide easily from prey among dead grasses. The lion's belly is a lighter color, sometimes labeled as a pale cream. The lion's tail is not as heavily furred and ends in a tuft of black hair, which conceals a sharp spur that actually comprises the last few bones of the tail. The lion's ears are also covered with black hair—sometimes inadvertently exposing the beast while it is otherwise camouflaged.

The body of the lion perfectly fits the needs of a predator. Its jaws are very large and have great power. The shoulders and forelegs of the lion are another source of great strength. In fact, among cats, the lion is matched only by the tiger in the power of its limbs. The lion makes great use of the force in its legs when hunting, using blows from its paws to knock down and weaken its prey. The paws are particularly large and include long claws, used as hooks to hold victims. Because the claws retract in the paws when not in use, they maintain their sharpness. The claws are also used to aid in eating, as the lion is able to remove excessively large chunks of meat from its teeth, with the claw serving in the manner of a toothpick. The lion's tongue is also suited for helping digestion, as it is well equipped for rasping meat.

Within the lion's mouth are thirty teeth. The four largest are the razor-sharp canine teeth, with which the lion is able to grasp and kill its prey. There are also four carnassial teeth, used by the lion for cutting through tough skin and other tough parts of its food, such as tendons between muscles and bones. There are no lion teeth that are able to chew food, and so the animal must swallow its food in chunks.

Of all cats, male lions are the only ones with manes. Not all breeds of lions have the same type of mane, however. Among surviving lions of India, there are both heavy and lightly maned males, and this was also true of several of the extinct breeds of lions, such as the Barbary and Cape lions. And some of the lions of Africa, particularly those in the Serengeti, have variations in the color and thickness of their manes. But for most males, all parts of the head, except the face, are covered with heavy, thick hair, as are the neck and the shoulders. The lion's mane is a great help during fights, because the thick hair considerably softens the blows of its foes. The male's mane is not fully grown until it reaches the age of five, though young males start to grow a little hair around their heads when they reach the age of one. The colors of the mane may vary from black to brown or yellow, with most manes having a mixture of these colors. As the lion gets older, the mane darkens.

Among the other distinguishing features of the lion are its amber eyes. They are considerably wider than the human eye, being more than 1.5 inches (37 millimeters) in diameter, compared to .9 inch (23 millimeters) of the human eye. But an even more distinctive and famous feature of the lion, and one that distinguishes it from all other species, is its loud roar. Under the right weather conditions, the lion's roar can be heard at distances of more than 5 miles (8 kilometers). To create such a sound, the lion normally needs to be standing, bending its head down slightly, and greatly expanding the chest. The roar of the lion has such power that it often stirs up great dust clouds.

Most of the roaring of the lion is done in the hour following sunset. Although roaring is such a distinctive feature, those who have spent time studying lions are still not certain of its true purpose. It could be a way of signifying control over territory. Or it could be a means of expressing contentment.

Lions make other sounds in addition to roaring. They sometimes utter low grunts as they walk along at a normal pace. They may give off a quite noticeable growl when they are angered. By contrast, a mother lion makes a soft sound when calling to her cubs.

Until recent times, it was assumed that lions did not climb trees, and it has been said that many people caught in vulnerable locations have saved themselves from lion attacks by staying in trees overnight. But further research into the subject has indeed revealed that lions do climb to very high perches in tall trees. And apparently, lions are capable of such climbing without much difficulty, because photographers who have taken pictures of lions way up in trees have noted unbent branches, indicating the ease with which the climbing occurred.

It's obvious that with the great strength of their limbs, lions are capable of springing distances both high and far. This is true even though lions are not as famous for their leaping ability as many other members of the cat family. But those who have studied lions close up have seen them jump long distances. The maximum leap of a lion has been measured at as much as 40 feet (12.1 meters). This knowledge perhaps should change the way lions are displayed in zoos and other exhibits, where they are normally kept from spectators by moats of about 30 feet (9.1 meters). It is likely that what keeps lions in those settings from jumping is their general dislike for water.

For all its majestic reputation, the lion is actually a rather lazy creature. Most of the animal's average day is spent resting.

THE LION'S WAY OF LIFE

Lions, much more so than any other members of the cat family, live sociable lives. They live in "prides," which are social structures including numerous lion members. The group can include up to thirty-five lions, but usually numbers somewhere from ten to twenty. Within this group, there are usually up to four nonpermanent males. The lionesses, who make up the bulk of the pride, along with their cubs, almost always stay in the same group for their entire lives.

Male cubs are generally expelled from the pride after three years. They either leave or are driven off by a different, usually younger, group of male lions. The cycle then repeats itself. Those driven off from a pride usually band together and roam until they reach the age of five, at which age they find a different pride, in which they are able to drive off the males and assume leadership themselves. Groups of male cats, normally numbering two to five, control the females and the territory. In the social structure of the pride, the weakest male is always thought of as higher than the strongest female.

Once they take control of a pride, the group of males works vigilantly to keep intruders, particularly other males, from disrupting the social structure. They also do not allow nonpride members to hunt in their territory. Intruders are warned to stay away from the area both by the roaring of the males and also by the liquid scent they leave on bushes. Any stranger who persists in the territory must then be ready for a violent fight. The male lions also put an end to disturbances that take place within the pride itself. The arduous nature of these tasks has resulted in the male lions only rarely

The lions in a pride can be very cooperative with one another. One example of this is the treatment of old, sick, or injured members. Healthier members often obtain food for those unable to do so.

taking part in the hunts for food, leaving most of that responsibility to the females. Studies have shown that the male lion hunts for only twelve percent of its own food; females supply it with seventy-five percent; and other predators' kills, which it simply takes, account for the remaining thirteen percent. As the percentages would indicate, male lions consume more than their fair share of kills made by females.

When the females hunt and gather food, they leave their cubs alone and abandoned in stretches that frequently last as long as forty-eight hours. Because of this, many of the cubs left behind and unprotected are often killed by hyenas, leopards, and even other lions.

Territory and Family Life

Each member of a pride does not claim its own territory, but rather all live in a single large area. A prime factor determining the size of the pride's area is the number of its members. Larger prides cover much more ground than do prides with smaller numbers. Because the range of areas inhabited by lions has become much smaller through the years, some pride territories overlap each other. This can lead to serious conflicts among the different prides, but generally the different groups are able to exist peacefully.

The degree to which food and water is plentiful determines how large an area each pride will cover. If there is abundant prey, the group usually covers an area up to 15 square miles (39 square kilometers). But if food is more difficult to obtain, the pride's territory may have to be

A lion pride often consist of two or three males and five to ten females, plus their young. Pride members generally coexist peacefully, but fights are most likely to erupt while feeding.

Two female lions are pictured in the process of bonding and grooming. Lions rub heads together to show that they mean no harm to each other. The greeting is often followed by several minutes of dedicated mutual grooming.

A resident of the Ngorongoro Crater, located within an extinct volcano, this lion lives in one of the most spectacular areas on the African continent. The crater is approximately 10 miles (16 kilometers) across and 5,000 feet (1,517 kilometers) deep.

These two females have gotten into a violent tussle. Fighting often occurs at mealtime, since food is divided according to the strength of each lion.

Lions do not commonly wash their own faces with their paws, the way domestic cats do. Thorough grooming by a lion is best accomplished with a social companion.

Following page:

The male members of a pride do not allow nonpride members to hunt in their territory. Intruders are warned to stay away by the roaring of the males and by a scent left on bushes.

expanded to 100 square miles (260 square kilometers). The movement of the group can also be affected by weather. During seasons of heavy rain, prey is normally scarce for the lions in the woodland areas, but much more available in the plains. This means that many of the prides have to alter their searches to cover a wider area because movements of their prey are much more erratic. During the dry season, however, pride movement is far more limited, as prey is more readily available.

The family life is generally quite a serene one, at least by the standards of the wild. There have been instances observed of lions within a pride fighting with one another, and even examples of one member of a pride killing another. However, these events are very much the exceptions, and not at all typical of lion family life. As a rule, members of the pride follow some very orderly procedures. When there is food available, lions are often able to eat peacefully without squabbling, unlike many other animals, although feeding time is the moment when fights most often occur. The reason for this is that the food is divided according to the strength of each member, with the strongest member eating the most food. The division of the meal is marked by hissing, smacking, and growling among pride members. But after eating, the lions again return to the normal tranquility of their lives. Even members who had confrontations during the feeding will then often show affection toward one another.

Female lions produce five or six litters in a lifetime. Both the male and the female initiate mating. The female signals willingness to mate by flicking its tail and rubbing against the male. The male makes its intentions clear with a snarling grimace.

Cubs follow their mothers in quests for food from about the age of three months. But they do not take an active part until they are six or seven months old.

Lions gather at a waterhole for a drink, carefully avoiding immersing themselves in the water, to which they have an aversion.

A pride of lionesses rests beneath a tree, saving their energy for the hunt under the cover of darkness.

Among lions, as with other species, the females are more inclined to settle down in a particular territory than the males. Female members of a lion group share a large territory rather than stake out individual domains.

Lions sleep or rest up to twenty hours a day. When they roam, they generally cover a range of about 5 miles (8 kilometers) a day. However, to procure food, they will, if need be, sometimes cover up to 15 miles (24 kilometers).

Rarely do lions gather together in the same locations of their territory, but they do know the other members of their pride, and on those occasions when they do meet, they exchange friendly greetings by rubbing cheeks, shaking heads, and grunting. The skin above the lion's eye gives off a scented secretion that pride members recognize when they rub heads with each other. The result is that all members carry a common smell by which they recognize one another.

Lions also groom each other when they meet. This is done by two lions licking the head and neck of each other. Their tongues are rough and strong and are ideally suited for cleaning and combing fur. This is needed in particular after a meal, when the lions are often covered with blood. The licking also helps remove dirt, as well as ticks and other parasites.

Most of the grooming takes place among the females and the larger cubs. The adult males do not take part in the social grooming, except on rare occasions, most likely because of the difficulty of cleaning the heavy hair of the male's mane. As for self-grooming, lions have difficulty maintaining a posture that frees paws to clean their faces. But they do keep the rest of their bodies quite clean.

Playing is another means of bonding among pride members. The male lions do not take part in much of the playing, while the females are much more frequent participants. This is another way lions are differentiated from other animals, specifically wolves and various wild dogs, whose females rarely are involved in such activities. Lionesses will playfully stalk and wrestle with other females, and they will also play considerably with cubs. This type of activity usually consists of the female poking a cub with its paw while the cub swats back, often while rolling on its back. Because they have not yet developed sufficient coordination, the youngest cubs taking part in the playing tend to do less running about and stalking, preferring just to grapple and roll about.

While most lions play in pairs, cubs also amuse themselves without companions. They often find sticks to carry and throw about, and this often leads to competitions with other cubs who try to capture the object themselves. Cubs are also known to try to play with the tufted tails of the adult males, though this frequently results in stern admonishment from their elders.

Another example of the cooperative nature of the pride is the treatment of old, sick, or injured members. Other, healthier members of the pride hunt food for those unable to do so. But when lions are old and very weak, they themselves become the prey of other carnivores, usually hyenas or wild dogs. As a result, lions in the wild do not survive to die of old age.

Lions Outside of Prides

Some males expelled from a pride do not seek to rule other prides. Instead, they continue to roam for their entire lives. They are often joined by many other younger males—who never attached themselves to prides or departed from prides at a very young age—as well as by many females, who make up about one third of the total of "nomads." Thorough research of these animals

A golden sunset on the east African plain catches this huge male lion in silhouette. Most lions are social creatures, but a percentage are unattached and nomadic.

in the wild has revealed that only about ten percent of these nomadic lions roam individually. The great majority of the nomads form groups, though they are much less rigid and organized than those of lion prides. Most of these groups consist of only a handful of lions. Some have as few as two members, while other groups of nomads have been documented to include as many as a dozen members, with possibly a few more.

Besides the number of members in each group, there are several other distinctions between the lions living as nomads and those living in prides. For example, there is no genetic relation between the members of a nomadic group, as there is in prides. And while many lions are part of the same pride for life, and most intruders are summarily

The lion's diet depends on what is available in the area it inhabits. If it cannot find the prey it favors—such as zebras, antelope, and domestic livestock—it will eat whatever it can find, including fish.

The dominant male lion in a pride maintains its position for a period of about eighteen months maximum. By that time, other aspirants to the throne will have almost inevitably given him a successful challenge. The ousted lion is sometimes killed in the process.

driven off, nomadic groups are not nearly as restricted. Members arrive or depart frequently, and new associations are also formed without conflict. Many of the contacts made by nomads last just a few hours, while others endure for a few days. Nomads frequently wander in and out of several groups during a short period. There is documented evidence that some nomads make contact with a half dozen or more lions within just a couple of days. With so many different contacts, each nomad soon begins to encounter previous acquaintances, which makes it even easier to form casual groups.

One of the most likely reasons for the open nature of nomads toward each other is that most of them are not territorial. There are some nomadic groups who do defend certain land areas, but this is not the case with most of them. And because they have no particular land to defend—unlike members of a pride—they are far less hostile to intruders, and in many cases, allow strange lions to join them in social settings and even to partake of meals.

Apparently, lions who are not territorial are much more tolerant of other lions, and studies in the wild have shown that though it may take some persistence, a nomad may well be accepted almost peacefully by other unattached lions and allowed to become a member of the casually formed and allied group.

This female lion is on the hunt. As lionesses hunt and gather food, they leave their cubs alone for periods as long as forty-eight hours. Because of this, many cubs left behind and unprotected are killed by hyenas, leopards, and even other lions.

Most lions live within a very structured social unit. An intruder into the family unit is often violently challenged. The fights that erupt sometimes prove fatal for the nonpride lion.

Lions often groom each other—a particularly practical habit after a meal, when the animals are often covered with blood. Mutual licking also helps remove dirt, as well as ticks and other parasites.

Because of the lack of good cover in scrub areas, the lion often has trouble catching its prey in daytime or on a night with a full moon. Prey can often detect the lion's presence from hundreds of yards away, enabling it to escape.

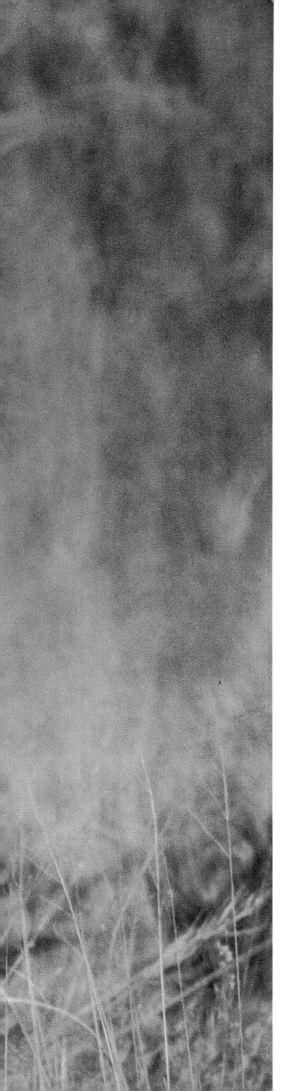

REPRODUCTION

Lions tend to breed throughout the year, though there are some patterns that have been observed. In the wilds of the Serengeti, as well as in South Africa's Kruger National Park, most breeding takes place from March to June. In western Africa, as well as India, the lions tend to breed from October to December. If the female does not become pregnant during these periods, another breeding cycle usually occurs within three months. During the times of mating, males and females are together constantly. The lionesses are in heat from four to eight days. Lions have been known to mate forty times a day, although even higher numbers have been counted. In a German zoo, two paired lions mated more than three hundred times in a week-long period. The actual mating itself only lasts about six seconds, which often concludes with the male lightly biting the female's neck, to which the female usually responds with a swing of her paw and a low growl.

The Role of Genetics

All the female members of a pride are closely related to each other, since all new members are the daughters, granddaughters, aunts, or nieces of the lionesses they replace. This means that all the offspring of the pride are also closely related, and so the male members who are driven out of a pride and take over another group are

Cubs stay dependent on their mothers for some time—often more than two years. When their mothers next mate, however, the cubs must fend for themselves. Lions reach their full size and strength by the age of five or six.

A male and female lion are shown in the act of mating. Because the lioness may mate with more than one male, it is biologically possible that members of the same litter may have different fathers.

also usually full brothers from the same litter. Because the female lion may mate with more than one male, it is biologically possible that members of the same litter have different fathers. There is also a chance that the partnered males of a pride may not have the same mother, although, almost always coming from the same pride, they are related, even if distantly. In sum, the males who are companions in controlling a pride may be full brothers or they may only be distant cousins, while all the females are usually closely related. However, the females are not related to the males, and this allows for a greater genetic mixture.

The manner in which males take over a pride through superior strength is one of the ways lions are able to improve the breed with each passing generation. The superior genes of the conquering males, which make them capable of taking over the pride, are bred into their offspring, as are the superior hunting skills of the prospering lionesses. The stability required by the females to rear their cubs successfully is also evident genetically and bred into subsequent generations. By the process of natural selection, the superior genes of the able male and female become more common with each passing generation, gradually decreasing the less productive parts within the genetic mixture of the species. Through this process, lions are able to continually produce high-quality replicas of themselves.

Though it may appear otherwise, this female lion is actually getting in the mood for mating. Growling, pawing, and biting are typical elements in a lion's mating dance.

In some areas, such as Ngorongoro Crater in Tanzania, lion prides are harmed by inbreeding. This occurs because a locale like the crater—difficult to reach from areas beyond—decreases the number of outsiders coming into a pride's gene pool.

Following page:

It is generally believed that lion cubs are blind at birth and that their eyes do not open for two to three weeks. But cubs have been observed opening their eyes even earlier.

Lions tend to breed throughout the year, though patterns do occur from pride to pride and place to place. In the national parks Serengeti and Kruger, for instance, most breeding takes place in the months of March to June.

42

A pair of lions engages in the mating ritual, complete with elements of violence. The manner in which male lions take over a pride through superior strength is one way that lions may improve the breed with each successive generation.

Actual mating between male and female lions lasts about six seconds. The encounter often concludes with the male lightly biting the female's neck.

Are lionesses good or bad mothers? The only conclusive answer, really, is a little of both. On some occasions, they defend their cubs to the death. At other times, lionesses neglect their young—possibly to the extent that they die.

Giving Birth

The gestation period for the female is between 105 and 115 days. When ready to give birth, the female seeks a site that provides protection from such factors as cold, excessive sunlight, wind, and moisture. In the dry season, most lionesses give birth near rivers or reeds. In the rainy season, the pregnant lioness seeks higher ground amid rocks or suitable spots in hills. Not only must the spot secured provide protection from nature and access to water, but it must also camouflage cubs from enemies. There may be occasions when the mother moves the location, and when it does so, it moves the cubs one at a time, carrying them in the mouth.

Most lionesses have litters of two to four, although in captivity some have had as many as nine. In the wild, it is unlikely that more than four cubs could survive: Since the mother has only four nipples, more than four cubs could not obtain sufficient nutrition. If more than four cubs were born in the wild, the stronger ones would soon outdistance the weaker siblings.

Seen here, a female lion and cubs feed on a harte-beest kill. Younger members of a lion pride drive the prey into a kind of ambush, while the lionesses make the kill.

The period when
a lion cub begins
teething can be
very dangerous.
The appearance
of permanent teeth
brings with it a
great deal of pain,
leaving the cubs
subject to infections
and fevers.

46

At birth, each cub is about 1 foot (30.5 centimeters) long and weighs about 1 pound (.45 kilogram). When they are born, lion cubs are already covered with fur and have some gray spots of varying shapes. They are also born with a wide, untufted tail. It is generally believed that lion cubs are blind at birth, and their eyes do not open for two to three weeks, though there have been examples spotted of eyes opening earlier. There is no evidence, though, that the cub's eyesight functions until three to four weeks after birth. Their milk teeth first appear about three weeks after birth, and they are able to start eating meat about one week later.

All the female members of a pride are closely related to each other, since all new members are the daughters, granddaughters, aunts, or nieces of the lionesses they replace.

Raising Cubs

After giving birth, a mother lion stays away from the other members of the pride for about six weeks before rejoining the group, with cubs in tow. When the cubs are old enough to move about on their own, several mothers often form a group. The responsibility of caring for the cubs is then shared by all the mothers. The cubs in this group do not just nurse on their own mother, but on anyone who is available. And the mothers protect all of the cubs as if they were their own. It is also not unusual for a female without cubs but with the pride also to shield and care for the cubs.

At birth, cubs are about 1 foot (30.5 centimeters) long and weigh in the area of 1 pound (.45 kilogram). When they are born, the cubs are already covered with fur and have gray spots of varying shapes.

The male lions in the pride also tolerate the cubs—even when the youngsters play with their food and even try to take food out of the adults' mouths. At most, the males show their disapproval to the young ones with a hissing sound.

Cubs begin to follow their mothers in quests for food at about the age of three months. But they do not take part actively until after they are weaned from the mothers, usually in their sixth or seventh months. Before that, their role in the hunting forays is more one of watching and stumbling along. A most dangerous time for the maturing lions occurs in the period between their ninth and twelfth months, when their permanent teeth first appear,

Lion cubs spend a lot of their time at play, grappling with and swatting one another. Their pawing and wrestling resembles the play of domestic kittens.

*A mother lion is not entirely selfless.
When food is scarce, the lioness will take
care of its own needs before those of the cubs.*

Although they have demonstrated a capacity for producing larger litters in captivity, a lioness seldom has more than four cubs at a time, for very practical reasons. Since the mother has only four nipples, more than four cubs could not obtain sufficient nutrition.

Though several lion cubs may die in a litter, the number that survives is sufficient to maintain a typical group's continued existence. Cubs born to nomadic lionesses have a harder time surviving.

In the wild, most female lions have litters of from two to four cubs. In captivity, this number has increased considerably, with some lionesses having as many as nine in a single litter.

On a family outing, lionesses and their cubs gather at a waterhole. A lioness stays away from other members of the pride for around six weeks after giving birth. It then rejoins the group.

When cubs are old enough to move about on their own, several mother lionesses may form a group. The responsibility for caring for the cubs is then shared by all the mothers.

When a female lion gives birth, it generally keeps the litter in a hiding place away from the rest of the pride.

Playing is an important social activity among lions. Adult males do not often take part in this, but lionesses and cubs play frequently. The animals stalk and chase each other, especially in the hours of dawn and dusk.

bringing with them a great deal of pain. The cubs in this period are subject to infections and fevers, as well as a dangerous level of restlessness. For these reasons, there is a high mortality rate during this period.

Most of the lions who survive the dangers and rigors of their first year continue to hunt with their mothers for quite some time, often more than two years. Mothers leave their offspring to fend for themselves when they next mate. Lionesses do not have another litter until their previous cubs are at least one and a half to two years old. They do not have offspring with them of varying ages, so the more mature cubs who have left their mothers tend to band together for awhile, until they reach their own sexual maturity, usually at age four. At that age, the males start to establish their own territories. The lion finally reaches its full size at age four.

At the Masai Mara Game Reserve in Kenya, this cub rests away from the midday sun. The cub's mother is visible in the background, resting but ready to defend its young in a moment if there is trouble.

Following page:

When they leave their mothers, lion cubs tend to band together, at least until they reach their sexual maturity. This occurs at around the age of four.

There is a very high rate of mortality for lion cubs born in the wild. In some studies, as many as sixty percent of the cubs died before reaching maturity.

A pair of Kenyan lion cubs is pictured at play. While most cubs play in pairs, the young ones also amuse themselves without companions.

Most of the lion cubs who survive the dangers and rigors of their first year in the wild continue to hunt with their mothers for some time, often for more than two years.

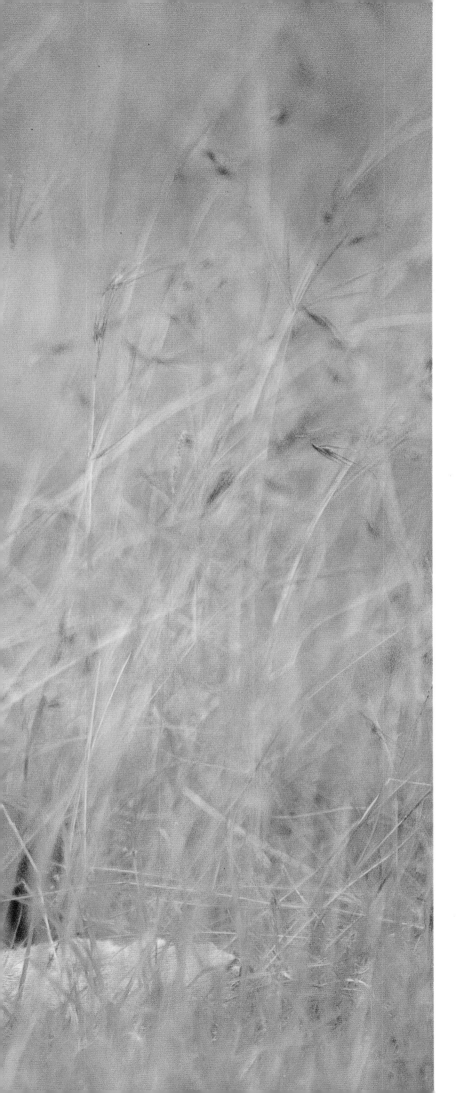

HUNTING

The choice of animals that the lion hunts for food is dependent on what is available in their areas of habitation. Generally, the scrub areas in which the lions live provide many animals who live off the vegetation of the region. These herbivorous animals—wildebeest, zebras, antelope, gazelles, and waterbuck—are the lion's primary sources of prey. They also have a fondness for warthogs, and have been known to wait many hours for them to emerge from holes in the ground. If a lion is hungry enough and otherwise not able to find food, it will also eat whatever it can find, including fish. Other larger animals are also hunted by lions, including buffalo and giraffes, though it is much more difficult for the lions to succeed in their attacks against these stronger creatures. Many lions have been injured trying to control the bigger animals. It's common after such an encounter for an injured lion to be unable to take part in any future hunts.

Most hunting done by lions is under a cover of darkness, when there is much less chance for them to be detected. It is common for the lions to observe their prey during daylight hours, usually soon before sunset. But they then wait until dark before attacking. Similarly, if there is bright moonlight, lions wait until it is obscured before they commence their hunts. Much of the reason for this is the lack of cover they have in their scrub areas of habitation. Often in the daytime, a lion will start to close in on a potential victim, but will be detected by its prey, who is then able to escape. Those lions who live in areas with more dense vegetation, however, are able to do more hunting in the daytime. Other hunting that occurs

A female lion guards its wildebeest kill. The lion's prey can depend on a number of natural factors. In some lion reserves, the wildebeest, for example, is not available during the dry season, when it migrates to the north.

This female has made its kill. In the Ngorongoro Crater, where this photograph was taken, geographical boundaries contain the wildlife, making prey plentiful and easy to catch.

The scrub areas in which most lions live provide prey in the form of herbivorous animals— wildebeest, zebras, antelope, gazelles, and waterbuck, among them.

Lions often make hunting for food a cooperative effort. In an attack, several lions encircle a herd, driving the victims into other lions, which await in the tall grass.

in sunlight is in relation to the activity of the lion's prey. When zebras or gazelles drink from lakes or rivers during the day, their presence often produces a flurry of hunting. But generally, most stalking by lions is done just after sunset, or, more commonly, in the middle of the night, several hours before dawn.

More than any of their other senses, lions use their sight to help them hunt. Lions observed under vegetative cover waiting to pounce give clear indications that their main way of following their prey is through vision. The best indication of this is when lions stick their heads up high out of their cover in order to follow the animal they are stalking. In the process they sometimes give themselves away. Final pursuit of a victim is also done strictly by sight.

Lions sometimes detect prey using their hearing. They frequently react to the sounds of animals walking or moving through water and set out to investigate. There have also been some examples of lions utilizing their sense of smell to aid in hunting. But generally, lions only hunt what they see, and they are not considered particularly adept at detecting prey. It is quite normal for a large group of potential victims to pass by during the day and not be noticed by sleeping lions.

In addition to the fact that their senses are not especially sharp, there are several other reasons that lions are not as proficient at hunting as other predators. Not only do they occasionally give away their cover, but they also pay little attention to the wind's direction, which frequently allows

A charging lion can reach speeds of close to 40 miles (64 kilometers) per hour. When a group of lions hunts together, its tactics are scientific and ruthless. The group encircles the prey, knocks it down, and then grabs and suffocates it.

At one time, the Indian lion could be found in a wide area across the northern part of the subcontinent. Today the 116 square miles (302 square kilometers) of Gir National Park and Lion Sanctuary is the only remaining home for the Asiatic animal.

It is lions versus warthog in this scene from the plains of Kenya. Most of a lion's prey can outrun it, so the big cat must stalk to within 100 feet (30.3 meters) before charging.

The bloody muzzle of this lioness indicates it recently made a kill. Greatly outnumbered by the animals upon which they prey—particularly herbivores—lions tend to actively hunt only one out of every fifteen types of species in their habitat.

their scent to be carried ahead, alerting potential prey to danger. However, despite some of the inefficiencies, prey is so plentiful in most of their current areas of existence that they are able to overcome these shortcomings. In their domains of eastern and central Africa, the lions are greatly outnumbered by the herbivores they hunt. Generally, they kill off about one out of fifteen of the zebras, gazelles, and other animals of the area. So the lions not only do not have much effect on the populations of their prey, but they also don't even help to control their numbers. The herbivores taken by lions through much of Africa only represent the amount that would be lost in the region's next drought.

In addition to the plentiful supply of quarry, other factors also help to make up for some of the lion's hunting deficiencies. Its inattentiveness to the wind often does not discourage

The lion is the largest of the African carnivores. While most of its prey is of medium size, it hunts and attacks anything from the tiny rodent to the enormous buffalo.

Lions descend on a buffalo kill, while other members of the buffalo herd look on helplessly. Though the lion triumphed in this confrontation, the buffalo, especially when wounded, is a fierce fighter. Indeed, many lions have been killed in battle with these sturdy animals.

This animal is stalking its dinner. Those lions who live in areas with more dense vegetation than the usual scrub are able to do more of their hunting in the daytime because they are more easily camouflaged.

While it is often written that male lions leave the primary hunting to the females out of arrogance or laziness, the male's heavy mane may have something to do with it as well. The mane makes stalking prey more difficult because it can be so easily spotted.

More than any of their other senses, lions use sight to help them hunt. Lions observed under cover waiting to pounce give clear indications that their principal way of following their prey is through vision.

Pictured in midhunt, a Kenyan lion closes in on its wildebeest prey.

Following page:

The average prey of a lion weighs about 250 pounds (112.5 kilograms). From this carcass, the lion obtains a meal of about 40 pounds (18 kilograms). Lions do not eat daily, although they have been known to hunt on days when they do not eat.

Lions often hunt alone, but also work cooperatively with several pride members to take on larger and stronger prey. During the attack, one lion suffocates the prey while the others move in to tear it open.

71

A lioness feeds on a buffalo kill. When females bring back food for the pride, the male lions take more than their fair share. About seventy-five percent of male lions' food comes from prey obtained by females.

An adult male drags a killed wildebeest across the dry grassland in the Masai Mara Game Reserve in Kenya. Every summer, millions of wildebeest migrate there from the drier regions of the south, keeping the lion population well fed.

One of the rare Asiatic lions of Gir National Park and Lion Sanctuary in India displays a bloody muzzle. The Asiatic lion is slightly smaller than the African type and has demonstrated a greater ability to coexist with humans.

potential prey from coming into sight, because during certain months of the year, the scent of lions is detectable by other wildlife throughout much of the region, especially by rivers or streams. So it would be impractical for gazelles or other herbivores to avoid water because they've picked up a lion scent.

Another, even more important reason that lions are able to find enough food is that they usually do their hunting in cooperation. They will stalk their victims for fifteen minutes up to an hour before pouncing. Normally, several lions circle around a herd they are attacking, driving their victims toward other lions hiding in tall grasses. These lions then attack their prey from the sides or from behind. This type of cooperative hunting also makes up for another notable problem that lions have, at least compared to many other predators: their lack of speed. Although lions are not slow,

Most hunting by lions is done under cover of darkness, when there is much less chance of their being detected. The lion pictured is stalking prey.

Several cycles of existence among Africa's wildlife are illustrated here: The predatory lions consume the wildebeest prey, while scavenging jackals and hyenas await their turn.

their maximum speed is about 30 miles (48 kilometers) per hour.

In addition, stamina is another problem for lions. They rarely run after another animal for more than 100 yards (91 meters). But by working in groups, they are able to capture prey that would otherwise be too fast or too elusive for them to catch.

Another advantage lions gain through group hunting is that when they have killed an animal too large for one to eat alone, several can take part in the eating. This not only gives food to more lions at one time, but also lets them avoid the problem of storing or guarding their food. Other members of the cat family, such as leopards or tigers, either hide their victims in trees or remain in the vicinity until they finish eating the carcass. Unlike the inhabitants of the jungles and forests, the lions in their scrublands would not be able to hide their food or shelter it.

Lions do not eat every day, although they have been known to hunt on days they don't eat. When a lion starts to eat, it usually begins with its victim's intestines, which is the most nutritious part of the meal. After that, the lion consumes the meat of the carcass, usually working forward from the hindquarters. The average prey of a lion weighs about 250 pounds (112.5 kilograms), from which each lion obtains a meal of about 40 pounds (18 kilograms).

If lions have had a really big meal, they usually rest for at least twenty-four hours. This is fairly common, because lions tend to consume whatever food they have, eating as much as 75 pounds (34 kilograms) of meat at one time. Prides have been observed gorging themselves for several hours and then moving very little for as many as four days. By the fifth day, they begin to walk around; by the sixth day, they are again ready to look for food.

The Masai Mara Game Reserve, established in 1961, is one of the best locations in the world for viewing big game in the wild. Among other facilities, the reserve offers visitors the chance to observe animals from hot-air balloons.

A male African lion transports an unusual prey—a crocodile. Crocodiles inhabit the pools in many game reserves, such as Nairobi National Park. The largest of the Nile crocodiles, growing to 16 feet (4.8 meters) in length, would not be easily vanquished by a lion.

This female lion, pictured with zebra prey, seems to be wondering if the photographer has designs on its dinner.

During a year's time, the hunting lion may kill about twenty animals. After the animal kills its prey, it is likely to begin eating the intestines, the most nutritious part of the menu.

THE LION AND MAN

The relationship between man and lion has been a significant one almost since the beginning of recorded history. Poets and artists, as well as royalty, rulers, and religious leaders, have long recognized the symbolic power of the King of Beasts.

Egyptian pharaohs and Assyrian kings kept lions as companions. Legend has it that these lions were trained to hunt and rode into battle with their royal masters. Ramses II, it has been written, went into combat with his prized great cat sharing his chariot.

Other rulers had crueler uses for their captive lions. In ancient Rome, lions were the wild beasts of choice for various horrible blood sports. In the great coliseums of Rome and elsewhere in the Empire, starved, maddened lions were pitted against each other or against equally desperate tigers and fought to the death for the amusement of spectators.

Still more bloody entertainment was provided by pitting lions against humans—either defenseless condemned prisoners (the early Christian martyrs among them), who were literally fed to the starving cats, or armed slaves and gladiators, who fought for freedom or riches. This latter spectacle has been immortalized in numerous histories, novels, and motion pictures. Such events would draw huge crowds of thirty thousand or more. The animals were kept in stone and

The lion's mane takes five years to fully develop. Young male lions begin to grow the mane at the age of one year, with a small crop of hair showing around the head at that time.

A lion track imprinted in the sands of the Kalahari Desert illustrates the impressive size of this animal's feet. The lion's huge front paws enable it to slap down prey with a brutal force.

As the spread of human populations overwhelmed them, lions were systematically eliminated from various parts of the world. Included in this group is the Barbary lion, which once roamed from Morocco to Egypt.

For nearly a century, Kenya allowed the nearly unrestricted hunting of lions for profit or sport. But by the 1970s, the country no longer tolerated poachers and trophy hunters. In 1977, Kenya made all lion hunting illegal.

steel cages, their fury rising as raw meat was dangled before them, always out of reach, and clubs descended on their heads.

The lion's designation as the King of Beasts can be traced back to writings from the first century. Lions were frequently part of royal family crests and coats-of-arms for the kingdoms of England, Scotland, Norway, Denmark, Wales, and Luxembourg. Richard I, the twelfth-century English king and veteran of the Crusades to the Holy Land, was dubbed Richard Coeur de Lion, or Richard the Lion Hearted, for his bravery in battle. The lion was frequently depicted as a symbol of power and strength in various parts of Asia—even in China, to which it is not indigenous.

The Lion on Display

In 1720, an African lion was the first foreign wild animal to be put on exhibit in North America. The exhibit caused a sizable commotion wherever it went. The owners used their lion exhibit to sell buttons and patent medicines. Following in the ancient tradition of rulers keeping lions at their side, American President Andrew Jackson accepted one of the big cats as a present from the Emperor of Morocco in 1830.

It was in the early nineteenth century that the first large-scale traveling circuses began to thrive in Europe and the United States. As in Ancient Rome, lions—typically billed as "Snarling Man-Eaters from Darkest Africa!"—were the highlighted stars of these spectacles, but unlike the Roman circus lions, these were not expected to maim and devour human beings at every performance. The key to a circus lion act was to make it seem as dangerous and exciting as possible without anyone actually being hurt. Skilled lion trainers, or "tamers," became international celebrities. The most notable of these early lion trainer stars was Isaac Van Amburgh, whose famous show was called the Grand Spectacle of Charlemagne. To the children and adults of several continents, he was known as the Greatest Lion Tamer in the World. Van Amburgh put on his lion act in legitimate theaters, as well as circus bigtops, and in 1839 he and Charlemagne, his lion, performed for England's Queen Victoria.

As the size and popularity of circuses grew, so too did their lion populations. The traveling show of P.T. Barnum in the 1850s—called Barnum's Great Asiatic Carnival, Museum and Menagerie—included up to ten lions in its featured act. Although tigers were an equally tempting attraction for most circus-goers, the Indian cats were much scarcer, being more expensive to import and more difficult to breed in captivity.

With no scientific manual for the training of wild animals, the early lion tamers learned their trade through a dangerous process of trial and error. In the first epoch of circus lion acts, the ideal was to present the animals in highly disciplined and formal tableaux, awing the audience with the sight of a human taming ferocious, man-eating beasts. But by the early twentieth century, American lion trainers were pioneering a new, more dangerous, and decidedly more exciting type of act. These trainers brought a glimpse of the violence of the African wilds, and a bit of the blood lust of the old Roman arenas, into the bigtop tents. The lion act became a frenzied drama, with groups of big cats wrathfully pacing the ringed enclosure, their trainer weaving among them with whip and upturned chair.

An African male lion engages in its most legendary characteristic behavior, a full-blooded roar. No one who hears that ground-quaking noise in person is ever likely to forget it.

A large African male lion is pictured resting. The lion's coloring allows it to blend in with the sandy-colored plain. The animal's belly is lighter than its top, which is a pale cream color.

The lion's mane is a great help during fights, because the thick growth of hair softens the blows of its foes.

A young adult female is pictured stretching. Although lions generally cover a range of about 5 miles (8 kilometers) in a day, they may cover three or four times that ground, if necessary, to obtain food.

Hearing the lions's roar on a recording does not prepare one for the vibrating force and power of a live encounter with this mighty sound.

Circuses reached their peak of popularity in the early twentieth century, with hundreds of different units, large and small, crisscrossing North America and Europe: the Cole Bros., Kelly-Miller, Sells-Floto, Al G. Barnes, Howe's Great London, Clyde Beatty, and, of course, Ringling Bros. and Barnum & Bailey, to name a few. Lion acts remained the leading attraction for most of these circuses, featuring as many as forty big cats in the ring at one time.

With so much competition, animal trainers were continually trying to increase the spectacle and danger in their acts. In the late 1890s, the European trainer Herman Weedon was the first to combine in one cage those traditional enemies, the lion and tiger. Other trainers followed his lead, intensifying their acts with hate-filled, danger-laden combinations from Africa and India.

While most trainers believed they were actually safer in a cage with a mixed-cat group (because the lions and tigers would be too preoccupied with each other to turn on the trainer), events inside the ring always had the potential to go completely out of control.

It is common practice for a lion to observe its prey during daylight hours, usually just before sunset. But the actual stalking and kill does not occur until darkness has fallen.

Lions reach maturity when they are between three and four years old. In the wild, the average life expectancy is about a decade. Pictured is a veteran lion on the Kenyan plain.

The Safari Years

While lions in captivity suffered confinement and humiliation and occasional abuse, many of the cats in the wild did not fare any better. The lion populations in Europe, Asia, and North Africa, as noted earlier, were almost entirely wiped out by hunting and human encroachment of their habitat. For all the symbolic value placed on the lion in the abstract, lions in the wild were effectively demonized as bloodthirsty man-eaters. Of course, in many of these cases it was only to be expected that the King of Beasts would put up a fierce fight when confronted with rifle-bearing intruders.

In the late nineteenth century, the time of the great African explorers, there were few who did not recount hair-raising encounters with a lion or two. Dr. David Livingstone had a near-fatal run-in while trying to help a group of Tswana tribesmen dispose of one rogue lion in the northern Transvaal. The traditional tribal method for trapping the animal involved spears and long fans made of bright ostrich feathers. As the hunters encircled and closed in on the lion, they would use the fans like matadors' capes, distracting and disorienting their quarry. On this occasion, the lion charged through the circle and hid in the nearby grass. As the group fanned out to search for the lion, Dr. Livingstone unfortunately stumbled upon its hiding place. Livingstone fired as the cat charged. The lion knocked the doctor flat on the ground, then climbed over him, took an arm in its mouth, and broke it. Livingstone was shaken so violently that he passed out. The lion was in the process of

These lions are about to make dinner out of an unlucky warthog. African lions were once routinely hunted and killed by tourists on safari. These days, the tourist is much more likely to watch the lion kill its prey.

dragging the doctor away when the tribesmen caught up and managed to kill it. The injury to Dr. Livingstone's arm plagued him for the rest of his life.

As the late nineteenth century in Africa was the era of exploration, the early twentieth century years were the time of the great hunting safaris (*safari* being a Swahili word for "voyage"). The change reflected the impact of colonialism. In less than twenty years, European claims on Africa went from ten percent of the total land mass to ninety percent. This brought tens of thousands of new settlers to the east African territories, and many of them were sportsmen and hunters, or at any rate eager to take a crack at the lion. The invention of inexpensive hunting rifles at the time made big-game hunting affordable for almost every European resident or visitor.

The growing number of newcomers and inexperienced hunters wishing to go into the wilderness

Once native to massive regions of Africa and the Middle East, lions were hunted down as human populations spread into their areas of existence. As a result, several subspecies of lions are now extinct.

Young male lions leave the pride within four to six months after reaching three years of age. They are then replaced by other males.

produced a need for professional hunters for hire. The safaris themselves grew to absurdly elaborate proportions, involving scores of bearers and supplies that ranged from portable bathtubs to pianos. The first-class African safari became de rigueur for the rich and powerful. Among those notables who went on lengthy lion-hunting safaris were the Prince of Wales, Lord Randolph Churchill, and U.S. President Theodore Roosevelt. Roosevelt's 1908 safari, recounted in his subsequent book, *African Game Trails*, did the most to popularize the large-scale African hunting expedition. The safari cost a staggering amount of money and involved a caravan of wagons, animals, and bearers stretched out for over 1 mile (1.6 kilometers) while on the move.

Roosevelt hunted the lion after the style of his adviser, Sir Alfred Pease, chasing the big cat down on horseback and then confronting it on foot for the kill. Roosevelt shot seventeen lions on this first safari—along with nearly five hundred other animals.

Some years later, writer Ernest Hemingway contributed to the romantic image of the big-game safari in such works as *The Snows of Kilimanjaro* and *The Green Hills of Africa*, based on his own experiences and observations in Africa. The lion hunt, in Hemingway's fictitious world, was a symbolic rite, the ultimate test of masculine courage.

On a less metaphoric—and less authoritative—level, Hollywood romanticized the safari as equal parts adventure and adultery. Lions were routinely, if excitingly, dispatched in these films, always

A beautiful female lion wades through a marsh in search of food. Lions enter water when necessary, but they do not particularly like it.

A lion may sometimes rest or sleep for an entire day after having a very big meal. This is understandable when one considers that a lion can gorge itself on as much as 75 pounds (34 kilograms) of meat at one time.

The body of the lion perfectly fits the needs of a predatory animal. Its jaws are very large and powerful. Among cats, only the tiger has a more powerful bite.

94

while furiously charging the hunters. Tarzan, Edgar Rice Burroughs' fictitious hero raised by African apes, was shown on screen in hand-to-hand combat with the lion. Tarzan was always the somewhat unlikely victor in these contests. The tamed, captive lions used in these movies were usually toothless senior citizens, and probably still capable of killing a stunt man with one blow of the paw if they weren't being such good sports about the absurd proceedings.

While writers and moviemakers glamorized the ritualized stalking and shooting of the lions, the reality was something else again. On actual safaris, the amateur lion hunters would frequently not make clean kills, wounding the cats and leaving them to the mercy of scavengers. Some hunters went after lions with packs of killer dogs. Although the east African authorities were strict about issuing limited-kill licenses for hunting elephants and other big game, lion hunting required no licensing at all: The King of Beasts ranked as vermin, to be killed at will without any need for authorization of limitations.

There is no way of calculating how many lions were killed in the fifty- or sixty-year "golden age" of the African safari, but it undoubtedly played an enormous part in the depletion of the overall lion population.

The Story of Elsa

The legendary Elsa of *Born Free* fame showed once and for all that lions are in fact adaptable and capable of crossing the boundaries between civilization and wilderness without dire consequences. It is a story worth recounting, as it did much to disprove negative perceptions of the lion.

The story begins with George Adamson, who became a game warden in Kenya in 1938. As the administer of an expansive area of over 100,000 square miles (260,000 square kilometers), which extended from Mount Kenya to the Abyssinian border, Adamson had the primary responsibilities of preventing poaching and taking care of animals in the area who posed threats to the people. In 1956, while seeking out a man-eating lion residing amid some hills in the region, Adamson was forced to kill a lion that attacked his group. It was only after the lion's death that Adamson sadly realized it was a nursing mother, and eventually he found its three lion cubs, which were hidden in a rock opening. He returned them to his camp, where he and his wife, Joy, began to raise them.

One of the lion's titles, King of the Jungle, is a misnomer. Most lions, such as this Kenyan male, live in grassy plains areas. They can exist both in colder areas and very hot regions.

Of the lion's thirty teeth, four canines are used for grasping and killing its prey. Four cheek teeth are used for cutting through tough skin and other tough parts of its food, such as tendons between muscles and bones.

Lions are not as proficient at hunting as many other predators. They reveal their cover at times, giving their prey time to escape, and pay little heed to the wind, allowing their scent to be carried ahead.

All three of the cubs were female, and, since they were only a few days old when they were retrieved, they had not yet opened their eyes. After a couple of days, Joy Adamson was able to get them to accept the unsweetened milk she offered them through a rubber tube. Soon, supplies arrived at the Adamson camp from the nearest African market, with more milk for the cubs, along with cod liver oil, glucose, and baby bottles. The cubs grew and soon began to partake of the normal lion recreations. They would stalk each other in the playful manner of lions living in prides in the wild, but with no adult lions around, they incorporated the humans at the camp into their activities, jumping on their backs as if hunting in the wild. The cubs would also climb trees, though often with such voraciousness that they ended up on too high a perch and needed to be rescued.

Their human handlers soon found out that the three female cubs all had distinctly recognizable personalities. Joy Adamson named one of them The Big One, another The Jolly One, and the third Elsa, after a friend of hers with a lively personality. If the three cubs had been raised in the wild, Elsa, being the smallest and weakest of the group, probably would not have been able to survive. But with the help of the Adamsons and the others in the camp, the cub not only survived but eventually prospered. The two stronger cubs were less reliant on handlers than was Elsa, and so they were sent to a zoo in Rotterdam, where they lived happily and luxuriously.

Elsa began to accompany the Adamsons on safaris in the wild. They traveled to many different areas of the continent. When Elsa was about two years old, the Adamsons allowed her to go off repeatedly on her own. Elsa did make other lion acquaintances. A half year later, the Adamsons decided to release Elsa back into the wild—an experiment that had never been attempted before with a lion raised by humans.

It was not easy, however, to wean Elsa from her human handlers. They attempted to show her how to hunt and kill, yet Elsa seemed reluctant to leave the couple to live entirely in the wild. She even became quite ill at one point. Eventually, the Adamsons found a different location for Elsa to live in—with a better climate, more accessible supplies of water, and no danger of hunters. In her new surroundings, the lion developed some hunting skills.

Finally, Elsa was able to be left on her own for a week. When the Adamsons returned to check on her, they found that her stomach was full, meaning she had eaten recently. Soon she took on a male lion partner. Eventually, as Elsa became more a part of nature with each day, she seemed all but ready to forgo all her great human friends in favor of her new, "natural" way of life.

As time went by, the Adamsons would still visit Elsa's area about every three weeks, firing off a shot to let her know they had arrived. Elsa would normally come into camp within a few hours and stay with the Adamsons for a few days. Amazingly, she was able to continue living in the wild while maintaining a relationship with the couple. They would always give her some meat on her arrival. When the Adamsons would be ready to leave, Elsa after showing much affection, would follow a routine of aloofness to lessen the pain of separation. The lion finally was able to lead an independent life.

The incredible experiment was a complete success. And it was made even more so when, late in 1959, Elsa gave birth to a litter of cubs. *Born Free*, written by Joy Adamson and published in 1960, chronicled the entire story. It startled the scientific community to the same extent that it entertained millions of readers.

The lion's differently shaped teeth are variously equipped for holding, killing, and cutting. As the lion has no teeth with which to chew, it must swallow food in large chunks.

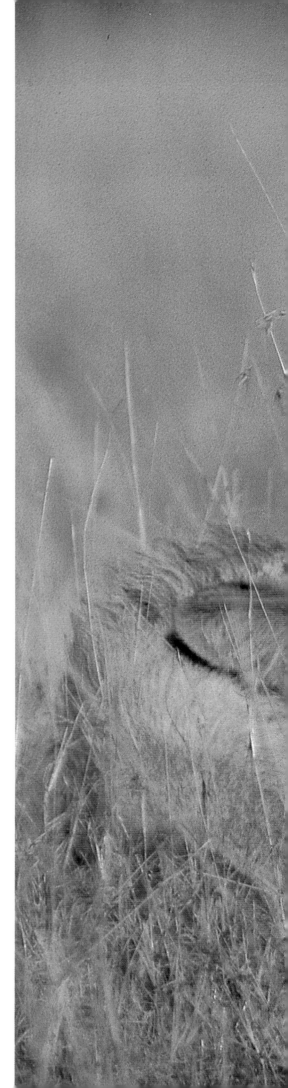

This fellow, a resident of the Amboseli National Park in Kenya, is showing why it is not a good idea to get within biting range of a wild lion: It is equipped with thirty teeth, some as sharp as razors.

Young male lions leave the pride within four to six months after reaching three years of age. They are then replaced by other males.

A TOUR OF LION COUNTRY

Progress and human overpopulation in this century have not mixed well with nature or wildlife. The roll call of vanished wilderness and extinct or endangered animals is a long one and still growing. The continent of Africa has faced this problem as much as any other. The usual elements—human encroachment, alteration or destruction of habitat, famine, excessive hunting, and poaching—have wiped once thriving species off the map in numerous regions of Africa.

At one time not many years ago, the world faced a future where such magnificent creatures as the elephant and the lion would no longer exist in the wild. Luckily, this situation was halted if not entirely reversed, by a combination of factors, from the growing strength of the conservation and ecology movement to African nations' awareness of the value of wildlife as a tourist attraction. In the past thirty years, the countries of Africa have gone to great efforts to reserve and protect their wildlife populations.

Now there are dozens of nationally sponsored game parks and reserves where the animal life thrives almost as it did before the arrival of civilization. In Kenya alone there are more than forty such areas. In most of these, there are facilities and accommodations for visitors on photographic "safaris" (the days of the huge hunting expeditions by tourists are now almost entirely illegal in the big-game regions of Africa).

Still, it is worth noting that no matter how large some of these animal reserves may appear to be, they are only a fraction of the land these animals once roamed freely. Kenya's vast system of national parks adds up to just over seven percent of the nation's total land area.

Because lions cannot adequately chew food, chunks sometimes remain their teeth. The claws are then used in the manner of a toothpick to loosen these pieces.

Each part of the lion's body aids its ability as a carnivorous hunter. Its jaws, teeth, shoulders, and legs are all sources of great strength. The paws are particularly large and are used to subdue prey.

Shimba Hills National Park is one of east Africa's coastal area reserves. It is located a short drive south from the city of Mombasa and contains, in addition to lions, a large elephant population.

The following tour highlights those areas where a permanent lion population can be found and visitors can generally arrange to observe the animals from some amazingly close vantage points.

KENYA

Kenya offers the visitor the greatest number of parks and tourist facilities for visitors, with reserves offering many chances for close observations of lions.

Meru National Park

Meru National Park has a special place in the hearts of lion lovers because of its association with Joy and George Adamson and Elsa, the *Born Free* lion. Lying along the equator to the west of Mount Kenya, Meru contains 320 square miles (832 square kilometers) of mostly semiarid land. At one time in the 1950s, the big-game population had almost disappeared,

Most lions live in what is termed "scrub country." This is an area made up of grassy plains and thorny scrub trees. But lions have also been found living at 2-mile- (3.2-kilometer-) high altitudes on Mount Kenya.

Following page.

Two females are shown at rest in Kenya's Masai Mara Game Reserve. The long siestas taken by lions are often a means of cementing social connections.

This female lion is climbing a tree in Kenya's Masai Mara Game Reserve. Despite their great size and weight, lions can move among tree branches without even bending them.

The wind coming over the Masai Mara Game Reserve in Kenya ruffles the mane of this elderly male lion. A lion's mane gets darker as it grows older. These stately animals can live into their twenties.

Although the lion is not the most efficient predator in the animal kingdom, prey is so plentiful in most of the areas where lions now thrive that they are able to find enough food without much trouble.

This male lion takes a refreshing break at a Kenyan waterhole. The travels of a lion pride can be determined by the availability of water and prey during the dry season.

but conservation efforts turned this situation around.

This area is very remote and difficult for visitors to reach. It is therefore very unspoiled.

Kora National Reserve

Bordering Meru and running along the Tana River, the Kora National Reserve is where the Adamsons together, and later George Adamson with his associate Tony Fitzjohn, worked on various lion projects. George Adamson spent many years at the dangerous business of trying to reintroduce captured lions to the wild. Tragically, he was killed by bandits in 1988, but research work with lions and leopards continues at Adamson's Camp. This area is devoted to scientific research rather than tourism, but visits can be arranged and good views of the lions are available for those with time and patience.

Female lions stalk through the grass at the Masai Mara Game Reserve in Kenya. Lions generally pursue prey as a group effort and follow their intended kill for fifteen minutes to an hour before pouncing.

Masai Mara Game Reserve

The Masai Mara is made up of the Kenyan side of Tanzania's Serengeti, and is therefore part of one of the greatest wilderness and wildlife reserves in the world. This reserve contains many sizable lion prides.

The lions are supplied with abundant and replenished prey due to the yearly migration of millions of zebras, wildebeest, and other animals traveling from the dry grasslands of Tanzania to the south.

The huge, open spaces of the reserve, covering 720 square miles (1,872 square kilometers), provides wonderful views of the lion populace. Facilities for visitors are very good, and there is the opportunity for touring the reserve from a spectacular vantage point in hot-air balloons, silently floating above the African plain.

In the Masai Mara Game Reserve in Kenya, vultures circle overhead, biding their time as they watch a lioness preparing to make a kill. After the lions finish feeding on the carcass, the birds will feast on whatever remains.

Nairobi National Park

The Nairobi National Park is amazing for its very existence, located as it is just outside the city limits of Kenya's capital, Nairobi. One can leave the crowded, bustling streets of Nairobi and in twenty minutes be nearby a lion pride, or zebras, wildebeest, cheetahs, and other wildlife. The capital city's modern skyline, with high-rise office buildings and hotels, is actually visible from various points inside the park. In a single moment it is possible to witness an ages-old scene of lion stalking prey while a jumbo jet aircraft crosses the horizon in the background.

Samburu National Reserve and Buffalo Springs National Reserve

These parks are in the dry, northern part of the country. The rugged, arid landscape means a mini-

Nairobi National Park is one of the most remarkable animal reserves in Africa, located as it is only 4 miles (6.4 kilometers) from the center of Kenya's capital city. One can actually see Nairobi's modern skyline from within the park.

This young lion is a resident of the Masai Mara Game Reserve in the east African nation of Kenya. Although it once thrived on several continents, the lion is now found almost exclusively in sub-Saharan Africa.

mum of covering vegetation, which gives the visitor clear views of the lion population. At the lodges here, it is often possible to see lions come very near to obtain bait.

Shimba Hills National Park

Shimba Hills is near the Kenyan coastline, 40 miles (64 kilometers) from the port city of Mombasa. The views through the rain forest along the coast are magnificent, but the small community of lions is found closer to the center of the park.

Tsavo (East and West) National Park

Encompassing 9,000 square miles (23,400 square kilometers), Tsavo National Park is a huge, rambling location with a variety of habitats, from marsh to mountains. Tsavo was once legendary for its huge elephant population and for the fact that the elephants were dyed red from the soil and dust in the park. Poachers have decimated the elephants over the past decade.

The lions of Tsavo are a relatively peaceful group compared to their relatives of a hundred years ago. At that time, the colonial government was building a railroad to Nairobi from Mombasa. The construction bogged down in Tsavo as countless railroad workers were attacked and eaten by the local big cats. The blood-curdling story was told in Colonel Patterson's *The Maneaters of Tsavo*, a bestseller in its day.

An early morning hunting party gathers in the Masai Mara Game Reserve in Kenya. The reserve, located along the Tanzanian border, is one of the best areas for observing lions and other big game.

Lions gather at the kill site in Tanzania. These animals do not kill in numbers that would affect the population growth of the prey in their habitat.

Accompanied by a cub, a lioness drags the carcass of a recent kill. Generally, a large kill means food for many lions at one time. The food is usually eaten quickly, rather than stored or guarded for future meals.

TANZANIA

Tanzania contains some of the most legendary wildlife reserves anywhere, from Serengeti and the fascinating Ngorongoro Crater, to Mount Kilimanjaro. In this region, lions roam over the sites of the earliest-known human fossil remains.

Lake Manyara National Park

Set along the Great Rift, Lake Manyara is a beautiful area of dramatic landscapes, with 130 square miles (338 square kilometers) of park land. Actually, most of that total is taken up by the lake itself, large portions of it covered by a million or more pink flamingos.

The lions here prove false the once widely held belief that lions do not climb trees. In fact, the Lake Manyara lions are often seen resting in acacia trees, whiling away their time until nightfall. The area is relatively unspoiled by human encroachment due to the prevalence of the tsetse fly.

A female lion stands beside the tall grasses of Ngorongoro Crater in Tanzania. Cut off from other areas by the walled-in crater, the lions are endangered by the increasing problem of inbreeding.

113

Lions like this one, a resident of Ngorongoro Crater in Tanzania, have been plagued by serious health hazards in recent years. A major problem has been the outbreak of tormenting, bloodsucking flies.

Mikumi National Park

An important area for wildlife researchers, Mikumi was made a national park in 1964, and is the third largest one in Tanzania.

The lions are most plentiful in the region north of the main road, along with herds of buffalo, hippopotamuses, elephants, zebras, and leopards. The lions here have gotten used to the presence of humans and vehicles in the area.

Ngorongoro Crater

Although it makes up only a small portion of the conservation area, the Ngorongoro Crater is the main attraction here. A crater within an extinct volcano, its 100-square-mile (260-square-

These animals are residents of the Ngorongoro Crater in Tanzania. The 100-square-mile (260-square-kilometer) floor of the crater is home to six separate lion prides. Naturalists have named each pride after aspects of the crater.

With their very strong limbs, lions can spring a great distance into the air—sometimes jumping into the boughs of trees.

kilometer) floor is home to six separate lion prides. Naturalists have named each pride after aspects of the crater.

The Ngorongoro Crater is in effect an island, cut off from the surrounding area. This isolation has had its good and bad points. The crater has one of the most congested wildlife populations in Africa, making the lions' search for prey quite easy. On the other hand, the islandlike setting has kept out newcomers and fresh genetic strains, leading to dangerous inbreeding. Over one hundred lions reside in the crater, while three thousand lions live in the Ngorongoro beyond the crater.

Ruaha National Park

Although it is Tanzania's second-largest game reserve, Ruaha is also remote and difficult to reach, and parts of it are completely cut off in the rainy season. Several lion prides can be found in the scrub and grassland areas of the park.

Serengeti National Park

The Serengeti National Park contains the greatest numbers of African big game anywhere on the continent. Serengeti stretches across nearly 6,000 square miles (15,600 square kilometers) of hills and plains. Vast herds of wildebeest, buffalo, gazelles, zebras, and others are spread across the area. The lion population enjoys such an abundance of prey that the prides seldom need to go outside their range.

The government has maintained the Serengeti without any of the more gimmicky tourist facilities and attractions offered at other reserves, thus making it the most unspoiled of all the great national parks in east Africa.

The lions of the Lake Manyara area of Tanzania are known for their tree climbing—and tree sitting. Some spend entire days perched in a comfortable tree branch.

This young male lion is a resident of South Africa's Kalahari Gemsbok. In this sanctioned habitat, the lion population thrives. Other reserves have not fared as well.

An African lion drinks from a waterhole in the Kalahari Gemsbok in South Africa. Dimly visible in the background is an approaching blue wildebeest.

SOUTH AFRICA

Colonialism in southern Africa in the early nineteenth century led to the extinction of at least one regional subspecies, the Cape lion, the last of which expired in the 1860s. Despite this loss, there are still other noteworthy lion-watching sites.

Kruger National Park

South Africa's largest game reserve is the last home of the Transvaal lion, a subspecies that was indigenous to the southeast tip of the continent.

Kalahari Gemsbok

The smaller of South Africa's main lion reserves, the stark landscape of the Kalahari allows for many unobstructed views of the big cats going about their daily lives.

OTHER AFRICAN COUNTRIES

Though not as well known as some of the other African wildlife parks, the following make for interesting lion-watching experiences.

Uganda: Queen Elizabeth National Park

Though threatened by civil war and other internal upheaval, this country has taken great care to nurture its massive wildlife population. In some places, however, poaching and neglect have definitely taken their toll.

Queen Elizabeth National Park is Uganda's greatest game reserve. Set against the Ruwenzori Mountains, it is a rich and beautiful region with a varied topography. For lion watchers, the place to go is the southern section of the park, called Ishasha. Difficult to reach at times, Ishasha is considered one of the most unspoiled game-viewing areas in Africa.

What distinguishes the lions in this 30-square-mile (78-square-kilometer) section is their propensity for climbing and resting in the local fig trees. It is not unusual to come upon a tree with two or three lions lazily perched in its boughs—a startling sight, and one seen on a regular basis only at one other game reserve, Lake Manyara in Tanzania. It is not certain exactly why the lions of Queen Elizabeth indulge in this habit. Some believe it is to escape the biting flies, which can be a major nuisance on the ground.

Ethiopia: Bale Mountains National Park

As in Uganda, political and social upheavals have threatened the wildlife preservation efforts in Ethiopia. Being a low priority on the government's agenda, the country's animals reserves are difficult to reach but well worth the effort.

The Bale Mountains National Park is Ethiopia's most important wildlife reserve, with a great variety of species and habitat. For viewing lions, one heads for the grasslands at Katcha. Few tourists come here, compared to the hordes that sometimes seem to turn the popular parks in Kenya into large-scale zoos. Visitors here are able to observe the lion populace under almost pristine, natural circumstances.

With sundown approaching, a grown male lion lies in repose in South Africa's Kalahari Gemsbok. Lions in the wild are now found chiefly in Africa's regulated game parks.

Following page:

The noble lion is pictured in a characteristic sphinx-type pose, photographed near sunset in Kalahari Gemsbok, a lion reserve in South Africa open to visitors.

Almost all remaining subspecies of lions are now African. Early in the twentieth century, the Indian lion population was down to barely more than a dozen. After being placed under protection by the government, there are now approximately 250 lions in India.

Rwanda: Akagera National Park

Rwanda is a densely populated, mountainous central-eastern African nation. This small country is better known for its mountain gorillas than its lion population. And, in fact, the lions of Akagera are not as reliable "performers" as those in the famed east African reserves, but Rwanda's lush setting makes the trip worth the effort.

INDIA

Gir National Park and Lion Sanctuary

Far removed from their African cousins, the lions of Gir are the only remaining colony of Indian, or Asiatic, lions. Even this enclave came very close to being wiped out and continues to have a questionable future due to the encroachments of humans and herds of grazing cattle, which force out the lion's natural prey.

The Gir population now stands at around 250. But visitors will find them far from elusive. The Gir lions have learned to live with the presence of humans and automobiles, so that close viewings by visitors are almost certain.

The park is closed during the monsoon season, and the best months for visiting are between December and May.

Although the lion survives in limited numbers in India today, it does retain a place of importance there. In fact, the lion is the emblem of the Republic of India.

Here is a rare glimpse of an Indian lioness, whose existence is now limited to a protected area of the Gir Forest in Kathiawar. The Indian lion was once threatened with complete extinction.

The Asiatic, or Indian, lion is smaller than the African version. Indian male lions also tend to have a more close-cropped mane. Despite their more diminutive stature, Indian lions are still quite mighty and magnificent animals.

Although they are now small in number, Asiatic lions have long been an important symbol in the Indian culture. The lion, known as the Lord of Beasts in Indian myth, was continually depicted as a symbol of strength and sovereignty.

At one time, the Indian lion could be found in a wide area across the northern part of the subcontinent. Today the 116 square miles (302 square kilometers) of Gir National Park and Lion Sanctuary is the only remaining home for the Asiatic animal.

THE FUTURE OF THE LION

The lion is here to stay—at least for the foreseeable future. Unlike so many other animals in this century, lions are not among those listed on any endangered species list, and none of the major remaining lion populations face any immediate threat of extinction. This is good news to be sure, although the idea that we can feel grateful that a creature has not been entirely wiped out indicates a woeful state of affairs in the natural world.

Parks, Reserves, and Wildlife Organizations

As it is, the wave of global interest in ecology, conservation, and wildlife protection that began to take hold in the 1960s came soon enough to give the African lion a new lease on life. Newly independent governments confronted two related facts: that tourism was a major or potentially major source of income for countries with large wildlife populations and, second, that the same wildlife was seriously in danger of being wiped out from hunting, poaching, and habitat encroachment. A nation anxious for income from tourism could no sooner afford to lose its lions than Miami, Florida, could afford to lose its beaches. The system of national parks and reserves began to develop, with game wardens and, where necessary, armed militia to protect the animals.

Other organizations, governmental and otherwise, including a number of nonprofit international groups—such as the African Wildlife Foundation, the Elsa Wild Animal Appeal, Wildlife Conservation International, the East African Wild Life Society, and the Worldwide Fund

A lion pride's territory and population can only expand if certain criteria are met. There must be enough game and water, as well as sufficient numbers of shady resting spots.

Several lion breeds survive today. The Masai lion lives in some of the protected areas of east Africa. The Senegalese lion lives in west Africa, along with other regional subspecies, including the Angolan, Rhodesian, and Transvaal lions.

for Nature—are among other organizations with programs specifically aimed at aiding Africa's healthy but limited population of wild lions thrive in the century to come.

One Possible Future

But the lion's "safety net" in the wild is not indestructible, and the future still holds pitfalls for this remarkable creature. The killings and habitat destruction of the past continue to affect the "protected" lion population of the present. The balance of nature is delicate, and once upset is not easy to set right again. When wilderness areas become fragmented, cut apart by human encroachment, the already-thinned lion populations become isolated. The number of potential mating pairs becomes smaller and the gene pool more limited. The long-term effects of inbreeding are an

A protected area for wildlife since 1948, Amboseli National Park was one of the first game reserves established in east Africa. Amboseli's open landscapes give visitors remarkable, unimpeded views of its lion population.

While now confined to Africa and a tiny area in India, lions were once plentiful in the Middle East and Greece.

The lion is one of the larger members of the cat family. It is distantly related to Felis catus, better known as the domestic cat, and shares many of the same characteristics of appearance and behavior.

This young adult is stalking its prey up a tree. Like other members of the cat family, the lion is a great leaper. There are reports of lions leaping as far as a spectacular 40 feet (12.1 meters).

Lions were once native to many parts of Europe, according to such evidence as cave paintings found in France. However, with the exception of Greece, they have not been found in the European wild since recorded history.

A lion in Botswana charges the photographer of this picture. Some tourists to Africa, apparently confusing game parks with zoos, take lethal risks in the presence of wild animals. Some tourists are attacked and a few killed by lions every year.

Once prevalent in ancient Greece, lions were described by Aristotle as scarce by 300 B.C. By A.D. 100 there were no further reported sightings of lions in Greece.

*The lion's scientific name is **Panthera leo**. It is sandy brown in color and is found in Africa and in India. Its closest relatives are the other majestic big cats: the tiger, the jaguar, and the leopard.*

increase in congenital defects, infertility, and a weakened immune system. When this occurs, a lion population—no matter how well protected within the boundaries of a national park—begins to shrink and deteriorate. It is a downward spiral that can mean the end of isolated lion groups, despite the best efforts of a government to hold off destructive acts.

The best test case for this potential "genetic erosion" in many lion reserves was observed in the Ngorongoro Crater in Tanzania. Animal biologist Craig Packer and his associate and wife, Ann Pusey, made a long-range study of the Ngorongoro's six lion prides, animals in a sense "marooned" on the 100-square-mile (260-square-kilometer) floor of the crater.

Their findings are that the isolated environment has fostered a series of circumstances leading to continued inbreeding. Through research and inspired detective work, Packer found that the Ngorongoro lions had gone through a number of cycles of reduced breeding population followed by genetic decline. First, hunters in the 1920s killed off a large percentage of adult males in a short span of time. Thereafter, a plague of bloodsucking flies reduced the lion populace to a handful in the early 1960s—the lions' susceptibility to the flies perhaps already indicated an immune deficiency from inbreeding.

Packer's research showed that the current population of one hundred or so lions in Ngorongoro are all descendants of just fifteen animals in the crater, and that the past five generations of lions were the products of close inbreeding. The crater lions were found to have lost considerable genetic diversity, having only half that of the less isolated Serengeti lions. Their reproductive rates were down, and they showed weakened immune systems. The potential for grave long-term effects on the crater lions may be a harbinger for the future of other lion populations locked within the boundaries of some animal reserves.

A more direct menace than inbreeding is the continued hunting and trapping of the African lion. Of the two east African nations with the greatest lion populations, Kenya continues to uphold a complete ban on lion hunting, but the government of Tanzania rescinded its ban in the 1980s, in order to increase revenues from foreign sport hunters. Difficult as it may be to believe, there are still people in the world willing to pay lots of money for the "privilege" of pointlessly shooting and killing a wild lion.

In addition to the animals lost to sport hunting, many lions are killed by poachers, mostly local tribesmen trying to trap animals for meat. The lions are inadvertently caught in the traps in these cases. Others trap and kill lions in order to sell body parts. Among some African tribes, the lion's claws and teeth are considered good luck talismans, while certain internal organs are thought to provide special powers when consumed.

This young male is ready for a catnap, using an uncomfortable-looking tree trunk as a pillow. Lions are often inactive, resting or sleeping for as much as twenty hours per day.

Following page:

Although lions are not slow compared to other animals in general, they are not as fast as many other predators competing for food in their habitat. The maximum speed of a lion is about 30 miles (48 kilometers) per hour.

A young African male lion yawns luxuriously. No matter how carefully the world's zoos try to simulate a natural environment, only in the wild can the lion experience the full range of its intended existence.

In a German zoo, a pair of lions was observed mating more than three hundred times in a one-week period.

Zoos

Once, not too long ago, zoos were considered nothing more than permanent exhibits, offering patrons a vivid glimpse of the exotic and dangerous creatures of the world's wilderness regions. Today, a zoo can be a scientific lab, a breeding center, and last refuge for endangered species no longer welcome in their homeland. In the past a zoo seeking to add a new lion to its collection would send for one to be captured and shipped from the wild. This is no longer feasible for various reasons, and so zoos have to create self-sustaining captive populations. Lions have bred very well in captivity, and all major and most minor zoos have them on exhibit.

Zoos have progressed greatly from bygone years, when animals were held in small, cramped cages. Today, zoos often create elaborate ambient enclosures, evoking the wilderness the animals came from with thick growths of vegetation, rocks, and waterholes. Nowadays as much attention is paid to the animals' psychological needs as to their physical needs.

Zoos attempt to create spaces with many visual barriers, giving the cats a chance to separate and not be face to face with each other at all times. Although lions do not hunt for their food in zoos, they are fed a raw, red meat diet similar to what they would devour in the wild, with the male being given slightly more than the female, as would occur in nature.

In the wild, the rigors of survival and the recurring necessity for hunting and catching prey keeps the lion's instincts sharp and mind alert. The captive lion can easily become bored and depressed from the lack of challenge, so zoos have to find ways of reactivating the cats' instincts and abilities. One effective method for accomplishing this is so-called environmental enrichment, in which new elements are brought into an enclosure and new challenges offered the lions. Keepers do what is known as "logpiling," in which food treats are hidden under piles of logs so that the cats must work to discover and then find them. Some zoos offer the lions "boomer balls," heavy-duty plastic balls containing similar treats inside. The balls are sometimes floated in pools of water—since the lions do not enjoy swimming, it means considerable mental concentration and physical effort to try and retrieve the balls without getting too wet. "You would be surprised how much good these little games can do, " says Craig Lewis, Senior Keeper at Washington Park Zoo in Oregon. "The challenge is very exciting for the lions. Something new, something to break up the day periodically, is as important to a lion's mental health and alertness as it is to a human's."

Zookeepers and animal researchers continually work to find new ways of challenging their captive population. Lions are traditionally one of the most popular attractions at any major zoo, but exhibiting is only one of the things zoos do with their resident lions. The breeding of lions, whether for captive propagation programs, or for the future necessity of reintroduction into the wild, presents special challenges for zoos. The bloodlines and genetic backgrounds of many captive lions are very tangled. As researcher Dr. Jill Mellen explains, "In the old days, it was not considered impor-

This beautiful cat displays its mighty paw. A lion's paws are extremely powerful, with very sharp, re-tractable claws.

Some African lions, particularly those in the Serengeti, have variations in the color and thickness of their manes. For most, the mane covers all parts of the head except the face and envelopes the neck and shoulders.

tant to keep records about the origins of particular lions. Asian lions were bred with African lions and so on. But for reintroduction to the wild, it would be inappropriate to put an Asian lion, say, into the African wild, or a lion of South African origin into east Africa." Zoos are now attempting to separate lions for breeding by assigned subspecies, under the assumption that a lion bred for a particular environment is most likely to thrive in that same environment.

But at the same time, they are conducting genetic research on lions to determine what exactly are the genetic differences.

Through the centuries, mankind has done much to honor the lion's existence and much to threaten it. We must hope that the future interaction of lion and man will emphasize the honor, and put an end to the threats.

Of all cats, male lions are the only ones with manes. However, not all breeds have the same type of mane. Indian male lions are both heavily and lightly maned.

During the dry season in east Africa, lion prides become concentrated along stretches of river. Though the prides often overlap, this usually does not present a serious problem.

The Barbary lion, one of several subspecies now considered extinct, could once be found from Morocco to Egypt. The last pure Barbary was shot in Morocco in 1920.

INDEX OF PHOTOGRAPHERS